Hairdresse

The Definitive Collection Of Hair Stylist Jokes

Published by Glowworm Press
7 Nuffield Way
Abingdon OX14 1RL
By Chester Croker

Jokes For Hairdressers

These jokes for hairdresser will make you giggle. Some of them are old, some are new, some are real highlights; so in this hairway to heaven, we hope you enjoy our collection of some of the very best hairdresser jokes and puns around.

FOREWORD

When I was asked to write a foreword to this book I was flattered.

That is until I was told that I was the last resort by the author, Chester Croker, and that everyone else he had approached had said they couldn't do it!

I have known Chester for a number of years and his ability to create jokes is absolutely incredible. He is an expert at crafting clever puns and amusing gags and I feel he is the ideal man to put together a joke book about our profession – he is simply a cut above others.

He will be glad you have bought this book, as he has an expensive lifestyle to maintain.

Jack The Clipper

Table of Contents

Chapter 1: Hairdresser Jokes

If you're looking for funny hairdressers jokes you've certainly come to the right place.

Here in this hairway to heaven you will find both corny hairdresser jokes and original hairdresser jokes crafted to make you smile.

We've got some great one-liners to start with, plenty of quick-fire questions and answers themed gags, some story led jokes and as a bonus some cheesy pick-up lines for hairdressers.

Chapter 2: One Liner Hairdresser Jokes

I don't know who keeps borrowing my scissors in this salon. But they need to cut it out.

You know you are a hairdresser when you can name at least five hairsprays by their taste.

A wife said to her husband “How do I look? I have just got back from the beauty salon.” and her cheeky husband replied “Was it closed?”

I asked the hairdresser to cut my hair like Elvis. The joker started wriggling her hips.

Customer: “Why did you take off so much of my hair?”

Hairdresser: “I didn't; nature beat me to it.”

Customer: “Couldn't you see I was going bald?”
Hairdresser: “No, the shine from your head blinded me.”

I told my last hairdresser loads of funny jokes. She dyed laughing.

I'm planning on opening up a combined waxing salon and cocktail bar. I am going to call it "Gin and Bare It".

Hairdresser: “Your hair is getting grey, Madam.”
Customer: “I'm not surprised with the amount of time you take fiddling about.”

I need to find a new hairdresser. I am fed up of this one talking behind my back all the time.

I went to a Jamaican hairdressers once.

It was dreadful.

Customer: “Why is my hairline receding?”
Hairdresser: “It's not. Your scalp is advancing.”

Some people get so touchy about their job titles. My young son's hairdresser doesn't like being called a child groomer.

I have decided not to visit that new Police Hair & Nail Salon. After all, you hear all kinds of bad things about Police Beautality.

Guess what I got asked when I was at the hairdresser's earlier on. Absolutely everything!

A blonde Australian tourist walks into a hairdresser's in London. “Did you come here to dye?” the hairdresser asks her. After a little pause, she replies “No, I came here yesterday.”

You know how they say you shouldn't run with scissors?

Well, you shouldn't scissor with the runs either.

The other day I walked into a hair salon. The receptionist said," How can I help you?" I told her, "I just need a short cut" as I walked across the salon and out through the back door.

My hairdresser doesn't cut my hair any longer. She cuts it shorter instead.

Did you hear about the narcoleptic hair stylist? She dyed in her sleep.

You know you are dating a hairdresser when he comes home with a bottle of wine and says “It’s Prom Season.”

You know you are a hairdresser when you don’t have to separate your laundry for the wash because all your clothes are black.

I hate the products that hair salons use for perms.

The smell just makes my hair curl.

I got called pretty today and it was a good feeling. Actually, the full sentence was “You’re a pretty bad hairdresser.” but I’m going to focus on the positive.

Customer: “Why doesn't my hairline look good?”
Hairdresser: “Because it’s on the same old head.”

Do you know why it is that ghosts always have long hair? It’s because all the hair salons are closed at night.

Did you hear about the hairdresser who stole a calendar? She got twelve months.

I found out my hairdresser had a second part-time job, working over at the racetrack.

She grooms horses.

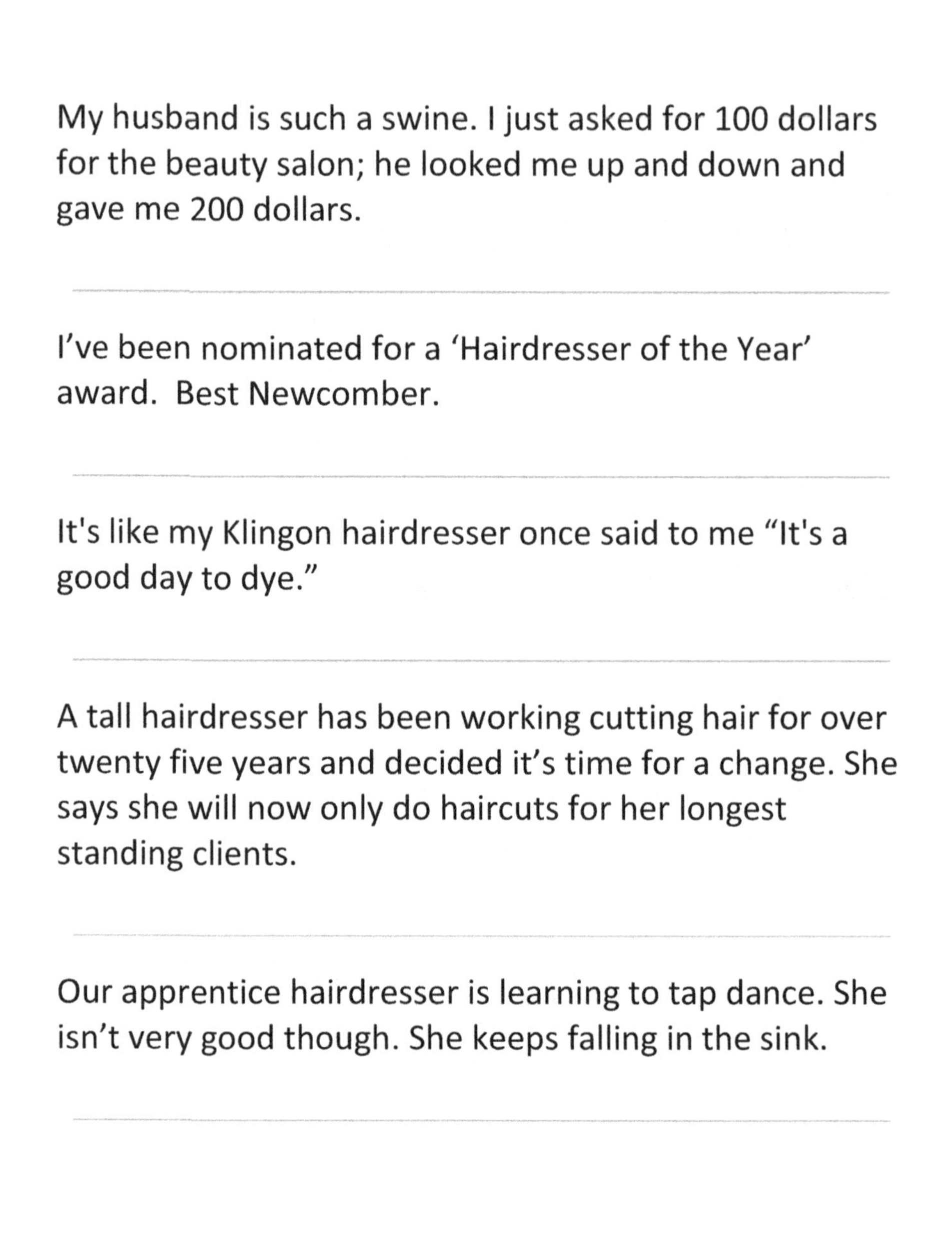

My husband is such a swine. I just asked for 100 dollars for the beauty salon; he looked me up and down and gave me 200 dollars.

I've been nominated for a 'Hairdresser of the Year' award. Best Newcomber.

It's like my Klingon hairdresser once said to me "It's a good day to dye."

A tall hairdresser has been working cutting hair for over twenty five years and decided it's time for a change. She says she will now only do haircuts for her longest standing clients.

Our apprentice hairdresser is learning to tap dance. She isn't very good though. She keeps falling in the sink.

A guy called Sherlock has just opened a salon in my town.

He has called the place Sherlock Combs.

I went to the hairdresser today and she asked me "Do you want your hair cut around the back?" I said "In here is fine."

I have to say that scissors really impress me. It is cutting-edge technology.

My job application for the senior hair stylist position was declined after the hands-on interview. I just didn't make the cut.

A wife asked her husband “Do you like my new haircut?” and her cheeky husband replied “Did a student trainee do it?”

I went to get my hair cut and told the stylist not to take too much off.

So she just took off her blouse.

My sister went to the hair salon and got rid of five inches. First of all, she got her hair colored and then she dumped her useless boyfriend.

A hairdresser friend of mine gave me some great advice, saying I should put something away for a rainy day. I've gone for an umbrella.

This one came out of a Christmas cracker: Question:- What do you call a line of men waiting for a haircut? Answer: - A barbecue.

I said to a male customer today "You've had the same haircut since the 1980s. Will you at least think about changing it?" He said "I'll mullet over."

I got a haircut last week.

I didn’t like it at first, but it’s growing on me.

A hairdresser in my area just got arrested for dealing drugs. I have been a good customer of his for years. I had no idea he was a hairdresser.

Bob Marley was always nervous about going to the hairdressers. He dreaded it.

I am going to open a hairdressing salon just for animals. We are only going to do hare cuts.

My hair stylist asked me what I wanted today. I replied, "Can you please just do something that makes me look sexy." She started drinking a bottle of wine.

I had to find a new hairdresser.

The last one wasn't cutting it.

I was held hostage at a hair salon once. It was a very hairy situation.

Did you hear about the cannibal hairdresser who got disciplined by his boss for buttering up the customers.

A man walks into a psychic hair salon, and the receptionist tells him “Say no more.”

A hairdresser wanted to buy something nice for the boss, so she bought him a new chair. Her boss won't let her plug it in though.

There was a robbery at my local hair salon.

The police are combing the area.

I was going to go to a redneck hairdresser today, but I changed my mind. I may have dodged a mullet on this one.

I walked into a room where men were wearing capes, expecting great things. Then I saw that it was a barbershop.

A hairdresser's husband passed her a super glue stick by mistake, instead of her lipstick. She won't be talking to him for a while.

Did you hear about the cross-eyed hairdresser who got sacked because she couldn't see eye to eye with the customers.

News: A car crashed into a hair salon yesterday afternoon.

We’re still waiting for the highlights.

Chapter 3: Question and Answer Hairdresser Jokes

Q: Why doesn't a hairdresser like long phone calls?

A: She likes to cut them short.

Q: What do you get if you cross a hairdresser and a bucket of cement?

A: Permanent waves.

Q: Why are hair stylists like psychopaths?

A: Because they like people to dye.

Q: Why do hair dressers make very good drivers?

A: They know all the shortcuts.

Q: What hair style do you give to a boxer?

A: Bobs and weaves.

Q: What kind of food do you eat while waiting in line for a haircut?

A: Barberqueue.

Q: What did the hair stylist do when the Beach Boys came on the radio?

A: Ba ba ba barber – ran.

Q: What do you get if you cross a wireless with a hairdresser?

A: Radio waves.

Q: If the Pilgrims came over on the Mayflower, how did all the hairdressers come over?

A: On Clipper ships.

Q: What did the impatient hair stylist say to her customer?

A: I think we need to cut this short.

Q: How does the hairdresser in the moon cut hair?

A: Eclipse it.

Q: What do you call a blonde who has her hair dyed brown?

A: Artificial intelligence.

Q: What do you call an overpriced hairdressing salon?

A: A clip joint.

Q: Why did the caring guy bring his sister's poorly dog to the salon?

A: He was trying to get her pedicure.

Q: What do you call a hairdresser working on a balding person?

A: An air stylist.

Q: What was the name of the online hair stylists?

A: E-Clips.

Q: How did Moses comb his hair?

A: He parted it in the middle.

One for the kids –

Q: Where does a sheep get a haircut?

A: At the baa-baa shop.

Q: What's a hairdresser's favorite kind of cruise vacation?

A: Cruising on a clipper.

Q: Why do men love dating hair stylists?

A: Because they think that three inches is six inches.

Chapter 4: Short Back And Sides

A guy went to the hairdressers, and was placed in a comfy chair.

A very attractive female hairdresser placed the cloak over him and got cutting.

After a few minutes she noticed that the cloak was moving up and down rhythmically around the area of his crotch.

Disgusted she whipped the cloak off him yelling "How dare you do that in my salon?"

The man looked up at her in amazement and held up a pair of glasses.

"I was just cleaning my glasses," he said, shaking.

A hairdresser shop in town put up a sign having a go at the upmarket salon down the street.

The sign said, "Why pay eighty dollars? We do haircuts for thirty dollars."

The upscale salon then put up its own sign stating, "We repair thirty dollar haircuts.

Three women were sitting in the hair salon chatting about their pet names for their men.

The first woman says ""I call my man Budweiser because his name is Buddy and he sure is the wisest man I ever met."

The second woman says "I call my man Southern Comfort, as he's from the South and he sure keeps me warm at night."

The third woman says "Well, I call my man Cointreau, as he's a fancy licker."

A man walks into a hairdressers and says "Can you give me a haircut, where you take out a big chunk right near the top, cut one side shorter than the other, make it uneven and jagged along the front and also a few bald spots on the back of my head?"

The stylist replies, "That's crazy! I can't do that."

The man retorts, "Why on earth not? After all, that's what you did last time!"

Whilst I was getting my hair cut I asked the hairdresser when would be a good time to bring in my three-year-old daughter.

Without hesitation, the stylist answered, "When she's ten."

A bystander saw a man laid flat out in front of a beauty salon and was ready to give some assistance when the man came to, and regained his consciousness.

The bystander asked, “What happened?”

The man rubbed the back of his head and said, “I don’t know. The last thing I remember, my wife had just come out of the salon and I remember saying to her, ‘Well, honey, at least they tried.’”

Hairdresser: And how old are you, little man?

Young Boy: Eight.

Hairdresser: And do you want a haircut?

Young Boy: Well, I certainly didn't come in for a shave.

Hairdresser “How would you like your hair cut?”

Customer: “Anything that will make me look good.”

Awkward silence.

Hairdresser: “Well, I can try.”

A greasy guy walked into a hairdresser's shop and sat in an empty chair.

"Haircut, sir?" asked the hairdresser.

"No, just an oil change please." he replied.

The hairdresser was anything but skilled, nicking his customer more than once with his straight razor.

After the shave, the customer asked him for a glass of water.

"Are you thirsty?" the hairdresser asked.

"No. I just want to see if my face leaks."

A lady was telling a friend about her experience at a new hairdressers saying "The hair style is fine but I didn't like the four-letter words she kept using when she was cutting my hair."

"What did she say?" her friend asked.

"Oops" the lady replied.

A hairdresser goes to the doctor with a hearing problem.

The doctor says, “Can you describe the symptoms to me?”

The hairdresser replies “Yes. Homer is a fat yellow lazy man and his wife Marge is skinny with big blue hair.”

A hairdresser took his cross-eyed dog to the vet.

The vet picked the dog up to examine him and said, "Sorry, I'm going to have to put him down."

The hairdresser said "Oh no! It's not that bad is it?"

The vet replied, "No, he's just very heavy."

I was telling my hairdresser about my bad luck with men, after having just been dumped by my boyfriend.

The hairdresser told me a regular customer of hers had recently told her she had just found out that her boyfriend was married.

I asked her how long it took to find that out, and my hairdresser replied "About five haircuts."

My uncle never goes to a salon to get his haircut, as his wife does it for him.

When I asked him why, he replied "I'm not paying for a poor haircut."

The redneck had never been inside a hairdressing salon. “I’d like one of them fancy hairstyles ma’am”, he said to the stylist.

“Sure”, she replied, “I’ll just have to wash your hair first.”

She shampooed once, and then started shampooing a second time.

“Hey ain’t you already done that?” he queried.

“We always shampoo twice” she replied, “and now I am going to use a conditioner as well.”

The redneck was blown away by all this fancy treatment and he asked, “Are you gonna do it again ma’am?”

“No” she explained, “I’m only doing this on one condition.”

Hairdressers often have to listen to customer’s gossip, but yesterday a regular client came in and as soon as I flung the cape around her neck, she said, "Now where did I leave off last week?"

A dog walks into a pub, and takes a seat. He says to the barman, “I would like a glass of red wine please.”

The barman says, “Wow, that's amazing - you should join the circus.”

The dog replies, “Why? Do they need hairdressers?”

A hairdresser is struggling to find a parking space.

"Lord," she prayed. "I can't stand this. If you open a space up for me, I swear I'll start going to church every Sunday."

Suddenly, the sun shines on an empty parking spot.

Without hesitation, the hairdresser says: "Never mind Lord, I found one."

A wife returns from the salon and tells her man, "Honey, I took your advice and got a new hair color, what do you think?"

Her guy replies, "I think you misunderstood what I meant when I said 'it's time to diet.'"

A man is out driving one Sunday when a hare jumped out in front of him, and is run over.

He stops the car to check if the hare is in fact dead.

His sexy blonde girlfriend passenger reaches into her purse; pulls out a spray can, and sprays it onto the bunny.

Within ten seconds the rabbit had jumped up on its feet, hopped about a bit, and then jumped back into the roadside bushes.

The guy's girlfriend said "I love this product – it's Salon Selectives Hair Spray and it's great at bringing back life to dead hairs and instantly adding bounce."

I saw a man running down the street with a cape on, so I shouted out, "Hey - are you a superhero?"

He yelled back, "No, I am doing a runner from the hairdressers!"

Chapter 5: Longer Hair Jokes

Ron is talking to his friends Jim and Shamus.

Jim says, "I think my wife is having an affair with a hairdresser. The other day I came home and found a pair of scissors under our bed and they were not mine."

Shamus then confides, "Wow, me too. I think my wife is having an affair with an electrician. The other day I found some wire cutters under the bed and they weren't mine."

Ron thinks for a minute and then says, "You know - I think my wife is having an affair with a horse."

Both Jim and Shamus look at him in complete disbelief.

Ron sees them looking at him and says, "No, seriously. Only the other day I came home early and found a jockey under our bed."

A woman was walking down the street when she was confronted by a grubby homeless woman who asked her for a couple of dollars for dinner.

The woman opened her purse, pulled out ten dollars and said "Will you spend this on a beauty salon instead of food?"

"Are you crazy?" replied the homeless woman. "I haven't had my hair done in at least ten years."

"Well," said the woman, "In that case I'm not going to give you any money. Instead, I'm going to take you out for dinner with me and my husband tonight."

The homeless woman was shocked saying "But won't your husband be angry if you do that? I know I'm dirty and I probably smell pretty ghastly."

The woman replied, "That's fine. I think it's important for him to see what a woman looks like if she stops going to the hair salon."

A passerby saw an old man on a street corner, crying his eyes out, so he asked him what was up.

The old man told him “I was a successful hairdresser, and I sold my salon to a man for loads of money.”

The guy says, “OK, so what’s the problem?”

The old man then says, “I own a very nice house with a swimming pool.”

The guy looks puzzled and says again, “OK, so what’s the problem?”

The old man wails and says, “I own a fast car.”

The guy once again says, “OK, so what’s the problem?”

The old man confesses, “Last month I got married to a 25-year-old model.”

The guy said once more. “What is the problem?”

The old man bursts into tears saying, “I can’t remember where I live.”

A leggy blonde bimbo walked into a hairdressers with her headphones on. She says to the hairdresser, "Do anything with my hair, but don't take the earphones off".

So, the hairdresser started to cut but was finding it pretty difficult, so she thinks "What could happen if I took the headphones off?", so she took them off.

The blonde dropped to the floor straight away in a panic attack.

The hairdresser was puzzled but wanted to know what was so important that the blonde was listening to, so she put the headphones on herself.

Out of the headphones she heard: "Breathe in, breathe out, breathe in, breathe out."

A hair stylist was making small talk with an old customer, who told her stylist she was going on vacation to Europe and was flying with United Airlines.

The hair stylist said "United are awful. The service is dreadful, the food is terrible, and they always lose your luggage. So, where are you going?"

"Rome" the woman replied nervously.

"Rome? That's an awful city. It's dusty, crumbling, over-crowded and full of pickpockets" said the stylist. "Good luck if you try to see the Pope. Waiting in that crowd with thousands of others all day just to catch a glimpse of him for a couple of seconds doesn't make any sense to me."

A few weeks later the customer came in for a tidy up and the same stylist asked her how vacation went.

The customer replied, "It was amazing. The flight was comfortable and on time, and none of my bags were lost. Rome was awesome, lots to see and do and the people were very friendly. The real highlight was that I not only saw the Pope, but I got to talk to him as well."

"What did he say?" asked the stylist to which her customer replied "I love your outfit, but who the f*ck does your hair?"

Four men were due to play tennis, and three had arrived and while they were waiting on the fourth to show up they started discussing their children.

The first man told the others how his son that started working as a used car salesman, but now owns a car dealership and is doing so well, just last year he gave a friend a brand new car as a gift.

The second man said that his son has his own construction firm having started work as a bricklayer's apprentice and that he's doing so well that last year he was able to give a good friend of his a brand-new home.

The third man boasts that his son has worked his way up through a stock trading company, and is now so successful that in the last month he gave a very good friend a large amount of shares in IBM as a gift.

As the fourth man joins them, the other three guys inform him that they have been discussing how successful their respective sons are, and are curious to find out how his son is getting on.

He tells them, "I'm not pleased with how my son has turned out actually. He is a hairdresser, and he recently announced to me that he is gay. However, looking on the bright side, he must be good at what he does, because his last three boyfriends have given him a car, a brand new house and some shares in IBM."

A group of hairdressers, all aged 40, discussed where they should meet for a reunion lunch. They agreed they would meet at a place called The Kings Arms because it had a great atmosphere.

Ten years later, at age 50, the hairdressers once again discussed where they should meet for lunch.

They agreed to meet at The Kings Arms because the food and service was good and there was an excellent drinks selection.

Ten years later, at age 60, the friends again discussed where they should meet for lunch.

They agreed to meet at The Kings Arms because there were plenty of parking spaces, they could dine in peace and quiet, and it was good value for money.

Ten years later, at age 70, the friends discussed where they should meet for lunch.

They agreed to meet at The Kings Arms because the restaurant was wheelchair accessible and had a toilet for the disabled.

Ten years later, at age 80, the hairdressers, now all retired, discussed where they should meet for lunch.

They agreed to meet at The Kings Arms because they had never been there before.

A young female hairdresser is sitting at the bar waiting for some friends, when a sweaty construction worker sits down next to her.

They start talking and eventually the conversation gets on to nuclear war.

The hairdresser asks the construction worker, "If you were to hear the warning sirens go off, and you know that you've only got 20 minutes left to live, what would you do?"

The construction worker replies, "That's easy -I'm going to make it with anything that moves."

The construction worker then asks the hairdresser what she would do to which she gently replies, "I'm going to keep perfectly still."

Chapter 6: Hairdresser Pick Up Lines

I make hair contact before eye contact.

You're giving me an extension.

I have some hair in my sink. It's yours if you want it.

Will you do something different to me?

95% of my arm strength comes from blow drying.

Want to see my tool?

There is nothing better than a woman's touch on your hair.

My parents wanted me to become a physiatrist or an architect so I became both. I became a hairdresser.

Chapter 7: Bumper Stickers For Hairdressers

Never ask a hairdresser if you need a haircut.

I can't hear you so I just hope you are not asking me any questions.

Your hairdresser's advice is more valuable than your shrink.

I play with scissors for the shear fun of it.

If you think it's expensive to hire a good hairdresser, just try hiring a bad one.

Chapter 8: Summary

That's pretty well it for this book. I hope you've enjoyed it. I've written a few other joke books for other professions, and here are just a few sample jokes from my plumbers joke book: -

Q: How are doctors and plumbers alike?

A: They both bury their mistakes.

Q: What do plumbers say to their customers?

A: Each time you flush a toilet, you put food in my family's mouth.

Q: What would you find in Superman's bathroom?

A: A Superbowl.

About the Author

Chester Croker has written many joke books and has twice been named Comedy Writer Of The Year by the International Jokers Guild.

Chester, known to his friends as Chester the Jester, once helped out at a hairdressing salon but he didn't make the grade – he simply couldn't cut it.

I hope you enjoyed this collection of hairdresser jokes, and I hope they brought a smile to your face. If you see anything wrong, or you have a gag you would like to see included in the next edition of this book, please do so via the glowwormpress.com website.

If you did enjoy the book, please leave a review on Amazon so that other hairdressers can have a good laugh too.

Thanks in advance.

Made in the USA
Monee, IL
05 November 2021